A Mother's Love
A Coloring Book for Mother's Day

Welcome to this coloring book celebrating the unconditional love of mothers everywhere! A mother's love is one of the most powerful forces in the world. It is a love that is strong, nurturing, and selfless. It is a love that never fades, no matter how much time passes or how many challenges arise.

In these pages, you will find beautiful illustrations that capture the essence of a mother's love. From tender moments between a mother and her child to everyday acts of care and devotion, these images will inspire you to reflect on the depth of the love that you have experienced from your own mother or maternal figures in your life.

Coloring is a wonderful way to express yourself and unwind. As you fill these pages with color, take a moment to think about the ways in which your mother has shown you love throughout your life. Whether it was a hug when you needed comfort, a listening ear when you needed advice, or a cheering voice when you needed encouragement, her love has undoubtedly played a role in shaping who you are today.

This coloring book is dedicated to all the mothers who give so much of themselves to their children, and to all those who have been touched by a mother's love.

May these pages bring you joy, gratitude, and a renewed appreciation for the incredible bond between a mother and her child.

Happy coloring!

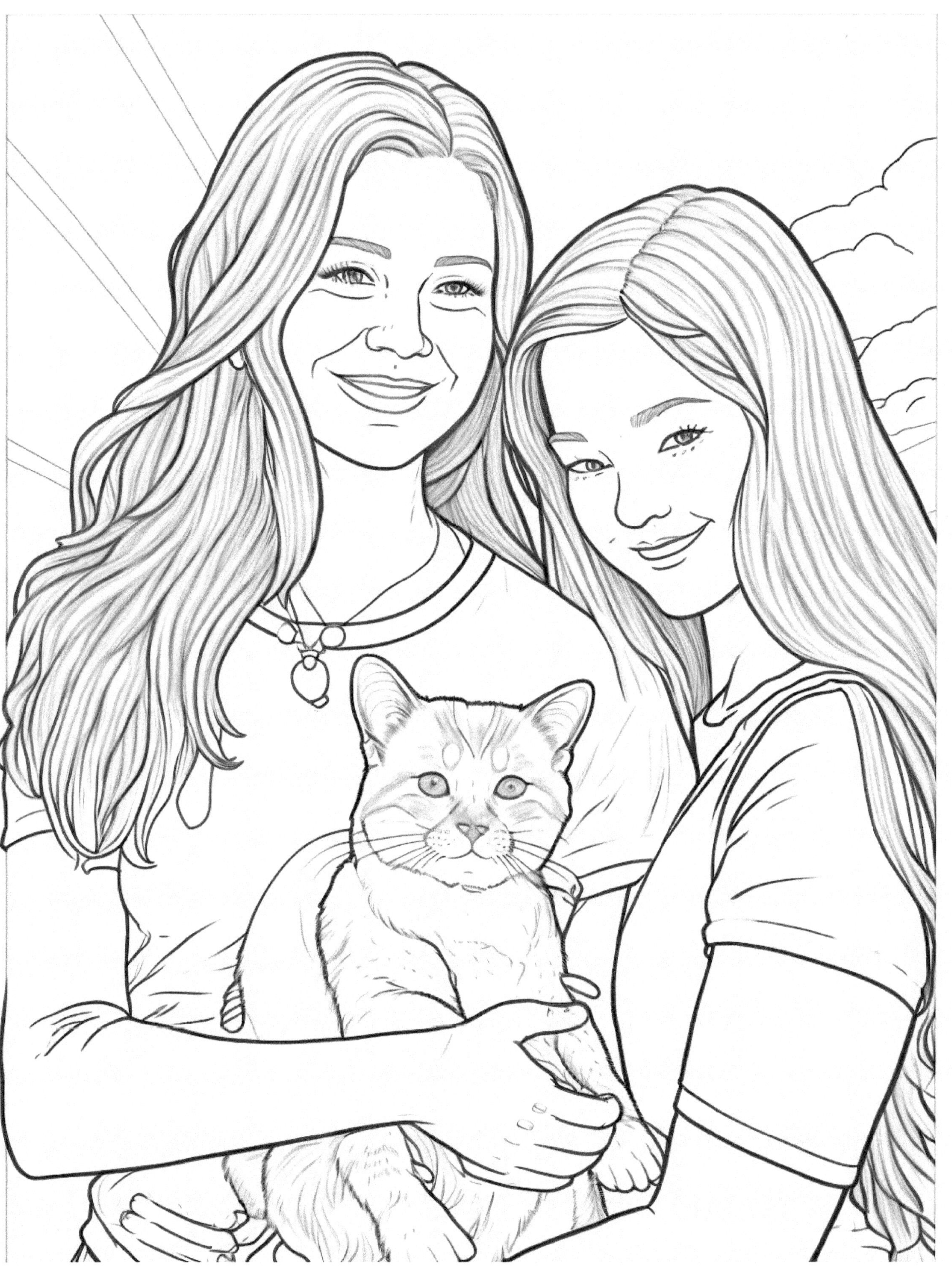

www.ingramcontent.com/pod-product-compliance
Lightning Source LLC
Chambersburg PA
CBHW081508250726
48662CB00012B/2710